STAR WARS™

WHAT IS A DROID?

Written by Lisa Stock

DK | Penguin Random House

Project Editor Katy Lennon
Designers Lisa Rogers, Jon Hall
Pre-production Producer Siu Yin Chan
Producer Mary Slater
Managing Editor Sadie Smith
Managing Art Editor Vicky Short
Publisher Julie Ferris
Art Director Lisa Lanzarini
Publishing Director Simon Beecroft

For Lucasfilm
Editorial Assistant Samantha Holland
Senior Editor Brett Rector
Image Unit Tim Mapp, Nicole Lacoursiere
Creative Director Michael Siglain

First American Edition, 2018
Published in the United States by DK Publishing
345 Hudson Street, New York, New York 10014

Page design copyright © 2018 Dorling Kindersley Limited
DK, a Division of Penguin Random House LLC
18 19 20 21 10 9 8 7 6 5 4 3 2 1
001–305823–Jan/2018

© & TM 2018 Lucasfilm Ltd

A catalog record for this book is available from the Library of Congress.

ISBN 978-1-4654-6753-9 (Paperback)
ISBN 978-1-4654-6754-6 (Hardcover)

DK books are available at special discounts when purchased in bulk for
sales promotions, premiums, fund-raising, or educational use. For details, contact:
DK Publishing Special Markets, 345 Hudson Street, New York, New York 10014
SpecialSales@dk.com

Printed and bound in China

A WORLD OF IDEAS:
SEE ALL THERE IS TO KNOW

www.dk.com
www.starwars.com

Contents

What is a droid?

Droids are robots.
They do jobs that are too
hard or dull for living beings.
Some droids are smart.
Some are useful.
Some are dangerous!

B-U4D
loading droid

4

MagnaGuard

R2-D2

R2-D2 has lots of useful tools. He can fly starships and fix them when they are broken. R2-D2 speaks in beeps.

R2-D2 carries tools to fix things.

Holoprojector

eye

feet with
wheels

C-3PO

C-3PO is polite and helpful.
He can speak lots of languages.
He does not like fighting.
He worries about getting hurt.
In fact, C-3PO worries
about everything!

Chopper

Chopper is a grouchy droid.
He works on a starship
called the *Ghost*.
He plays pranks on the crew.
They do not think he is funny!

Chopper zapping Ezra

dirty
paint

booster
rocket

long
arms

chest
armor

12

K-2SO

K-2SO is a tall droid.
He used to be scary,
but now he is friendly.
He helps his master,
Cassian Andor.

Cassian and K-2SO

DROID JOBS

Droids are built to make life easier for living beings. Here are some of the jobs that they do.

LABOR DROIDS

Labor droids can do many jobs, such as digging and cleaning.

Example: MSE-6
These "mouse droids" clean starships.

MEDICAL DROIDS

Medical droids treat life-forms when they are injured.

Example: GH-7
GH-7 performs tests to work out what is wrong with its patient.

MILITARY DROIDS

Military droids work as soldiers. They fight in battles and are hard to beat!

Example: Droideka
Droidekas are good at destroying things!

BB-8

BB-8 helps his master,
Poe Dameron, fly his X-wing.
BB-8 has been in many battles.
He helps Poe carry out
top secret missions.

BB-8 and Poe Dameron

antenna

eye

Dangerous droids

Super battle droids are
big and strong.

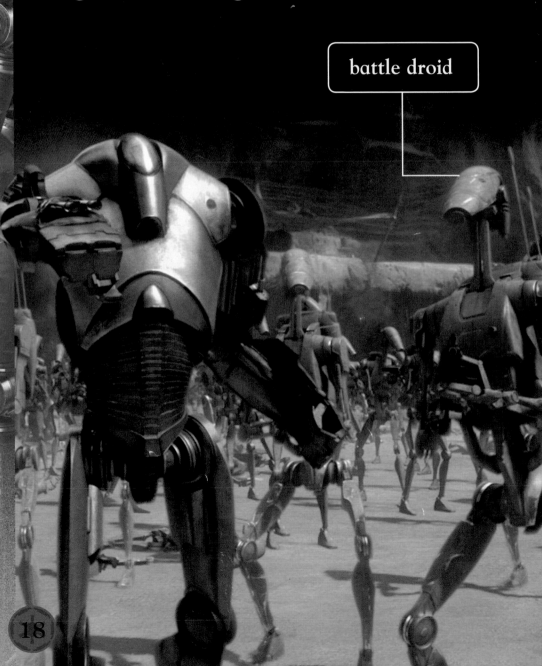

battle droid

They are built to destroy.
You do not want to get
in their way!

super battle droid

Quiz

1. What is a droid?

2. What does Chopper like to do?

3. What are super battle droids built to do?

4. How does R2-D2 speak?

5. Who is K-2SO's master?

6. What is the name of the ship that Chopper works on?

7. What does C-3PO worry about?

8. What type of droid is a droideka?

9. Who is BB-8's master?

10. What do mouse droids do on starships?

Answers on page 23

Glossary

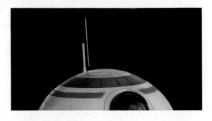

Antenna
A device used to send and receive radio signals.

Grouchy
Behaving in a grumpy or bad-tempered way.

Holoprojector
A device that projects images.

Living beings
Creatures that are born, unlike droids, which are made.

X-wing
A type of starfighter that has X-shaped wings.

Index

Quiz Answers
1. A robot 2. Play pranks 3. Destroy! 4. In beeps
5. Cassian Andor 6. The *Ghost* 7. Everything!
8. A military droid 9. Poe Dameron 10. Clean

A LEVEL FOR EVERY READER

This book is a part of an exciting four-level reading series to support children in developing the habit of reading widely for both pleasure and information. Each book is designed to develop a child's reading skills, fluency, grammar awareness, and comprehension in order to build confidence and enjoyment when reading.

Ready for a Level 1 (Learning to Read) book

A child should:

- be familiar with most letters and sounds.
- understand how to blend sounds together to make words.
- have an awareness of syllables and rhyming sounds.

A valuable and shared reading experience

For many children, learning to read requires much effort, but adult participation can make reading both fun and easier. Here are a few tips on how to use this book with an early reader:

Check out the contents together:

- tell the child the book title and talk about what the book might be about.
- read about the book on the back cover and talk about the contents page to help heighten interest and expectation.
- chat about the pictures on each page.
- discuss new or difficult words.

Support the reader:

- give the book to the young reader to turn the pages.
- if the book seems too hard, support the child by sharing the reading task.

Talk at the end of each page:

- ask questions about the text and the meaning of the words used—this helps develop comprehension skills.
- read the quiz at the end of the book and encourage the reader to answer the questions, if necessary, by turning back to the relevant pages to find the answers.

Series consultant, Dr. Linda Gambrell, Distinguished Professor of Education at Clemson University, has served as President of the National Reading Conference, the College Reading Association, and the International Reading Association.